Longwood Gardens

A Journey Through the Seasons

A JOURNEY THROUGH THE SEASONS

Longwood Gardens®

BECKON BOOKS

AT THE AGE OF 36, PIERRE S. DU PONT
PURCHASED THE PEIRCE FARM AND BEGAN CREATING
WHAT WOULD BE CALLED LONGWOOD GARDENS.

DU PONT CONSTRUCTED
LONGWOOD'S FIRST FOUNTAIN IN 1907.

In 1906, Pierre S. du Pont—industrialist, conservationist, and philanthropist—purchased a small farm near Kennett Square, Pennsylvania, to save a collection of historic trees. These preservation efforts soon evolved into a passionate commitment to gardening. Du Pont turned his farm into one of the great gardens of the world. Longwood Gardens now features unique garden displays and diverse programs in horticulture, education, and the performing arts. Longwood is committed to the values of environmental stewardship and community engagement.

Today, guests can experience the gardens through a series of unique events that highlight the beauty of each season.

THE CRISP WINTER MONTHS OFFER
A PEACEFUL VIEW OF PAULOWNIA ALLÉE
FROM ACROSS THE COW LOT.

7

EACH JANUARY, GARDENERS TRANSFORM THE CONSERVATORY FOR ORCHID EXTRAVAGANZA.

8

ORCHID EXTRAVAGANZA FEATURES A WIDE VARIETY OF ORCHIDS THROUGHOUT THE CONSERVATORY.

RARE BLUE-POPPIES—WHICH TYPICALLY GROW IN
COOLER CLIMATES—BLOOM EVERY MARCH.

THE MEDITERRANEAN GARDEN IN THE
CONSERVATORY INCLUDES SEVERAL PEPPER-TREES
THAT BEND OVER A STONE WALKWAY.

THE PEIRCE-DU PONT HOUSE SERVED
AS A WEEKEND RETREAT FOR LONGWOOD'S
FOUNDER, PIERRE S. DU PONT.

PRIDE-OF-TENERIFE AND BIGLEAF HYDRANGEAS BLANKET THE EAST CONSERVATORY.

ORCHIDS, ELEPHANT'S-EARS, AND PALMS
SURROUND THE REFLECTING POOL IN THE
CONSERVATORY'S TROPICAL TERRACE.

THE EAST CONSERVATORY FEATURES
AN ARRANGEMENT MADE FROM MOTH ORCHIDS.

FLOWERING CHERRY TREES ARE
AMONG THE FIRST SIGNS OF SPRING.

EVERY OCTOBER, MORE THAN 100,000 BULBS ARE PLANTED FOR THE SPRING TULIP
DISPLAY IN THE FLOWER GARDEN WALK, WHICH SPANS 600 FEET.

Purple tulips blanket the Flower Garden Walk.

Foam-flower and creeping phlox color
the landscape in Peirce's Woods.

AN EXQUISITE POPPY-FLOWERED ANEMONE
IN BLOOM IN THE IDEA GARDEN.

THE PERENNIAL BORDER IN THE IDEA GARDEN
INCLUDES IRISES, ORNAMENTAL ONIONS, POPPIES,
MOUNTAIN BLUETS, PEONIES, AND RHODODENDRONS.

A CORAL ROSE IN BLOOM DURING LATE SPRING.

FOXGLOVE USHER IN THE WARM WEATHER.

JAPANESE WISTERIA VINES ARE TRAINED INTO
TIERED TREE FORMS IN THE WISTERIA GARDEN.

During Lilytopia, the Conservatory showcases the newest varieties of lilies developed by Dutch breeders.

LONGWOOD'S ROSE ARBOR
BURSTS INTO BLOOM IN JUNE WITH
TRAINED RAMBLER ROSES.

A TROPICAL WATERLILY ON DISPLAY.

SANTA CRUZ WATER-PLATTERS,
AQUATIC CANNAS, LOTUS, AND WATERLILIES
IN THE OUTDOOR WATERLILY DISPLAY.

PIERRE S. DU PONT DESIGNED THE MAIN FOUNTAIN GARDEN
AFTER VISITING THE GREAT GARDENS OF ITALY AND FRANCE
AND SEEING HYDRAULIC DISPLAYS AT SEVERAL WORLD'S FAIRS.

THE 61-FOOT TALL
CHIMES TOWER HOUSES
LONGWOOD'S 62-BELL CARILLON.

A LOTUS BLOOMS IN THE WATERLILY DISPLAY.

MANY DIFFERENT CATEGORIES OF PLANTS—INCLUDING SUMMER ANNUALS—ARE GROWN IN THE IDEA GARDEN.

THE SQUARE FOUNTAIN GARDEN
IS SURROUNDED BY A SEASONAL DISPLAY
OF NEW GUINEA IMPATIENS.

The Italian Water Garden includes pruned littleleaf linden trees and clipped English ivy.

THE FIREWORKS AND FOUNTAINS SHOW ILLUMINATES THE NIGHT SKY.

A RAINBOW OF PUMPKINS AND GOURDS IN THE IDEA GARDEN.

LONGWOOD'S MEADOW IS
COVERED WITH WILDFLOWERS—INCLUDING
GOLDENROD—IN EARLY FALL.

THE TOPIARY GARDEN FEATURES YEWS FASHIONED INTO GEOMETRIC SHAPES.

THE CANOPY CATHEDRAL—ONE OF THE GRAND TREEHOUSES AT LONGWOOD—WAS MODELED IN THE STYLE OF A NORWEGIAN CHURCH.

THE LOVE TEMPLE AND LARGE LAKE
ARE SURROUNDED BY PEIRCE'S WOODS.

THE COW LOT AT LONGWOOD GARDENS IS BORDERED BY FALL FOLIAGE,
INCLUDING A MAJESTIC AMERICAN ELM TREE.

Autumn leaves on a Japanese maple tree in Frog Hollow.

DURING THE CHRYSANTHEMUM FESTIVAL IN THE FALL,
HORTICULTURAL EXPERTS TRAIN PLANTS INTO SPIRALS,
GIGANTIC HANGING BASKETS, ARCHES, AND CASCADES.

BIRD FOUNTAINS IN THE INDOOR
CHILDREN'S GARDEN ALLOW YOUNG
VISITORS TO SPLASH AND PLAY.

MORE THAN 20,000 MUMS ARE ON DISPLAY
DURING THE CHRYSANTHEMUM FESTIVAL, INCLUDING
THE THOUSAND BLOOM, MADE UP OF 1,000
PERFECT BLOOMS ON ONE PLANT.

POINSETTIAS, WINTER-FLOWERING
BEGONIAS, AND PAPER-WHITE NARCISSUS BLOOM INSIDE
THE ORANGERY DURING THE HOLIDAYS.

ILLUMINATED FOUNTAINS
DANCE TO FESTIVE MUSIC THROUGHOUT
THE HOLIDAY SEASON.

THE EXHIBITION HALL FEATURES
INNOVATIVE DISPLAYS EACH YEAR,
SUCH AS A CRANBERRY BOG.

THOUSANDS OF RED AND WHITE POINSETTIAS, BEGONIAS,
ENGLISH IVY, PINE CONES, AND MOSS CARPET THE
EXHIBITION HALL DURING A LONGWOOD CHRISTMAS.

THE EAST CONSERVATORY HOUSES MANY HOLIDAY TREES, INCLUDING
LONGWOOD'S 25-FOOT DOUGLAS FIR CHRISTMAS TREE, DECORATED WITH HAND-BLOWN
GLASS ORNAMENTS, PAINTED BRANCHES, AND THOUSANDS OF LIGHTS.

Longwood Gardens

Longwood Gardens is the living legacy of Pierre S. du Pont, inspiring people through excellence in garden design, horticulture, education and the arts.

In 1906, industrialist Pierre S. du Pont (1870-1954) purchased a small farm near Kennett Square, Pennsylvania, to save a collection of historic trees from being sold for lumber. Throughout his life, Mr. du Pont indulged his passion for gardening, turning his farm into a magnificent horticultural showplace. Today, Longwood Gardens is one of the world's great gardens, encompassing 1,077 acres of display gardens, woodlands, meadows, fountains, and a grand 4.5-acre conservatory, along with notable residential instruments like the 10,010-pipe Aeolian organ, a 62-bell carillon, and a 1923 Steinway grand piano.

From its origins, Longwood Gardens has made it a priority to teach environmental stewardship and to educate tomorrow's horticulture leaders. The garden settings have also long served as the backdrop for showcasing top performing artists. Since Pierre S. du Pont first welcomed his good friend John Philip Sousa to the Open Air Theatre stage in 1922, Longwood has hosted some of the finest artists from various performing genres. For more information, visit www.longwoodgardens.org.

Editorial Contributors: Kristina Aguilar, Tomasz Anisko, Marnie Conley, Patricia Evans, Jennifer Fazekas, Colvin Randall, James S. Sutton, Aimee Theriault, and Deborah Webb

1001 Longwood Road
Kennett Square, PA 19348
610.388.1000
www.longwoodgardens.org

BECKON BOOKS

Longwood Gardens: A Journey Through the Seasons was developed by Beckon Books. Beckon develops and publishes custom books for leading cultural attractions, corporations, and non-profit organizations. Beckon Books is an imprint of FRP, Inc., 2451 Atrium Way, Nashville, TN 37214. FRP, Inc. is a wholly owned subsidiary of Southwestern, Inc., Nashville, Tennessee.

Christopher G. Capen, _President, Beckon Books_
Monika Stout, _Design/Production_
Betsy Holt, _Editor_
www.beckonbooks.com
877-311-0155

ISBN: 978-1-935442-08-0
Printed in Canada
10 9 8 7 6 5 4 3 2 1

Photo credits:
Larry Albee: _2–3_ , _6, 7, 8, 10, 11a, 11b, 12, 13, 14–15, 16, 17, 18a, 18b, 19, 20, 21, 22a, 22b, 23, 24, 26–27, 28, 29a, 29b, 30, 31, 32, 33, 34, 35, 36, 37, 38–39, 40, 41, 42, 43a, 44a, 44b, 45, 46, 47_
Candy Bakey: _25, 43b_
Courtesy of Hagley Museum and Library: _4a, 4b, 5_
Terence Roberts: _9_